1. Birds of the Sea

Can you find your way from the seabird in the sky to the sunken 'Albatross' in the sea? Stay on the light blue path.

ALBATROSS

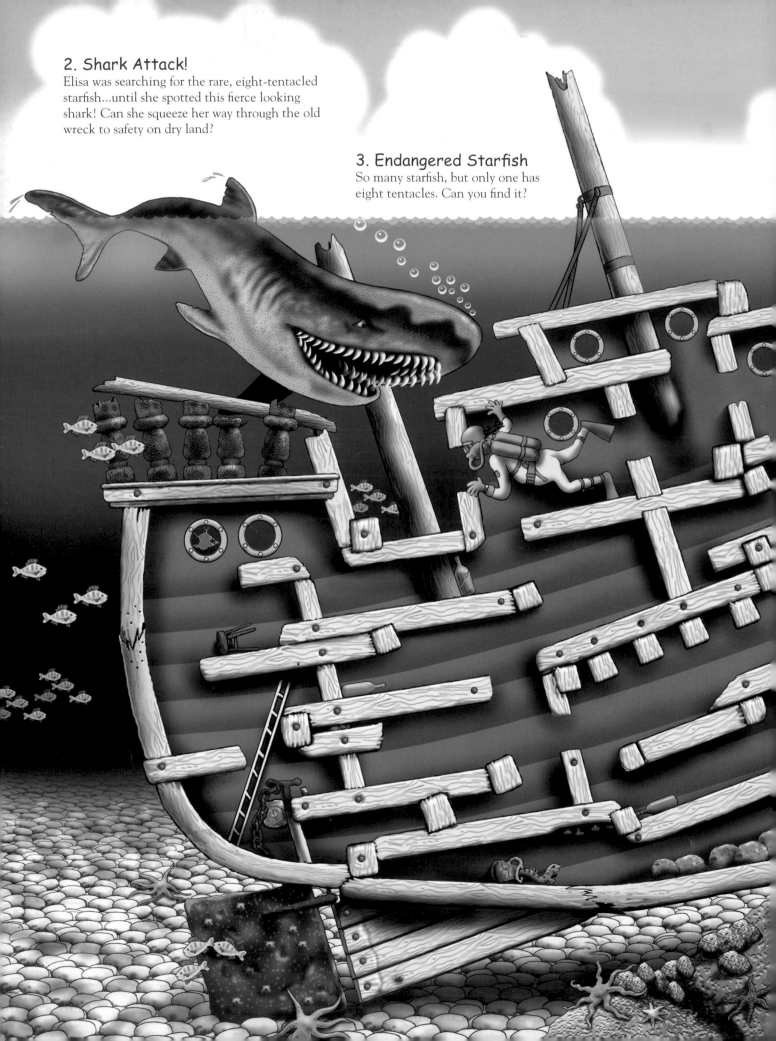

2. Shark Attack!
Elisa was searching for the rare, eight-tentacled starfish...until she spotted this fierce looking shark! Can she squeeze her way through the old wreck to safety on dry land?

3. Endangered Starfish
So many starfish, but only one has eight tentacles. Can you find it?

The Underwater Puzzle Book

AQUA MAZE

Rolf Heimann

www.littleharebooks.com

Little Hare Books
8/21 Mary Street, Surry Hills
NSW 2010 AUSTRALIA
www.littleharebooks.com

First published in 2009

National Library of Australia
Cataloguing-in-Publication entry

Heimann, Rolf, 1940-
Aquamaze: the underwater puzzle book / Rolf Heimann.
Surry Hills, N.S.W. : Little Hare Books, 2009.
978 1 921541 02 5 (pbk.)
Maze puzzles--Juvenile literature.
793.73

Designed by Bernadette Gethings
Produced in Singapore by Pica Digital
Printed in China through Phoenix Offset

5 4 3 2 1

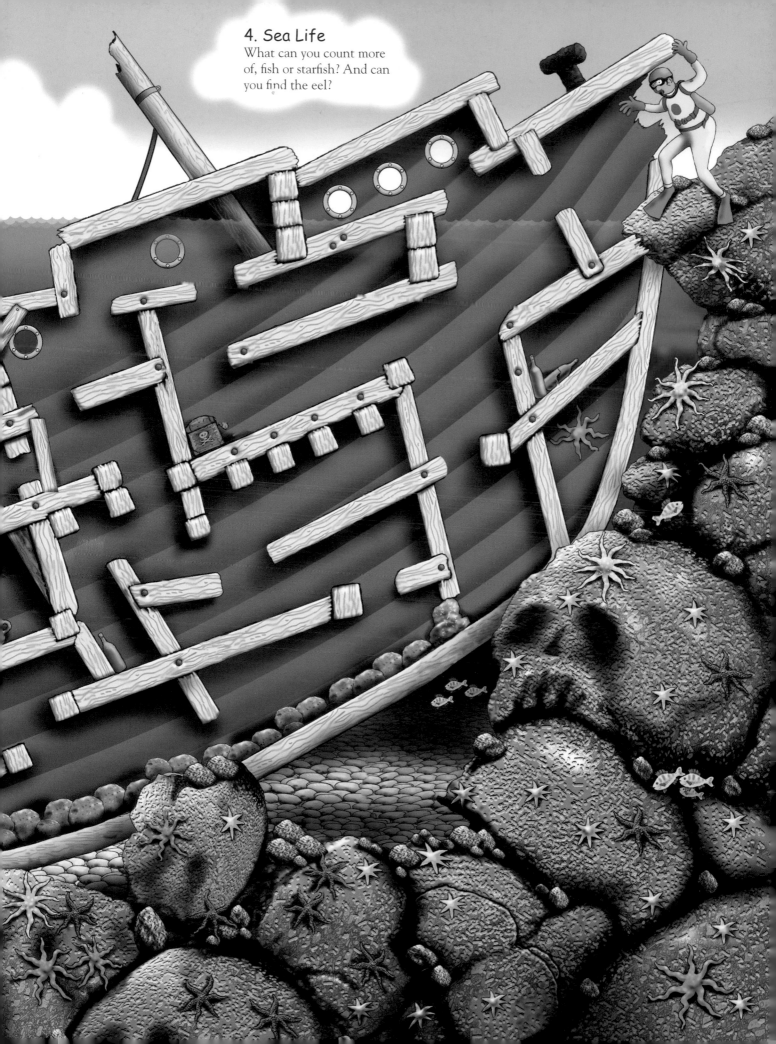

4. Sea Life

What can you count more of, fish or starfish? And can you find the eel?

5. Mind Your Step!

There are thirteen differences between these two pictures. Can you find them?

6. Dinner Time!

Can you help this little red fish find a worm for dinner? He'll need to swim quickly to beat the other fish!

7. The Lost World of Atlantis

Could these underwater ruins be a part of the legendary Atlantis? Make your way from one tower to the other before one of the purple octopuses gets you!

8. Octopus Maze
Can you help this sleepy octopus through the maze to his hole?

9. The Right Suit
It is important in an underwater race to have the right equipment. The grey diving suit is the cheapest, the green suit costs twice as much as the grey suit and the blue divers spent the same amount on their suits. Together the blue divers spent $300. Altogether the five divers spent $480 on their suits. How much did the grey suit cost?

10. Fish Racing

Even more important than your diving suit is the speed of your fish!
The two striped fish are the fastest. The fish marked '1' is the slowest and
the fish marked '4' is half the speed of the fish marked '5'. Which fish
will end up in the middle of the race?

11. Hidden Treasure

These two explorers are looking for a long-lost treasure chest. Will they be able to get to it?

12. Girl Meets Boy!

The spotted cod have an interesting lifestyle. Males and females live in separate underwater caves and only come together once a year. Finding the connecting tunnel is not easy. Can you help them?

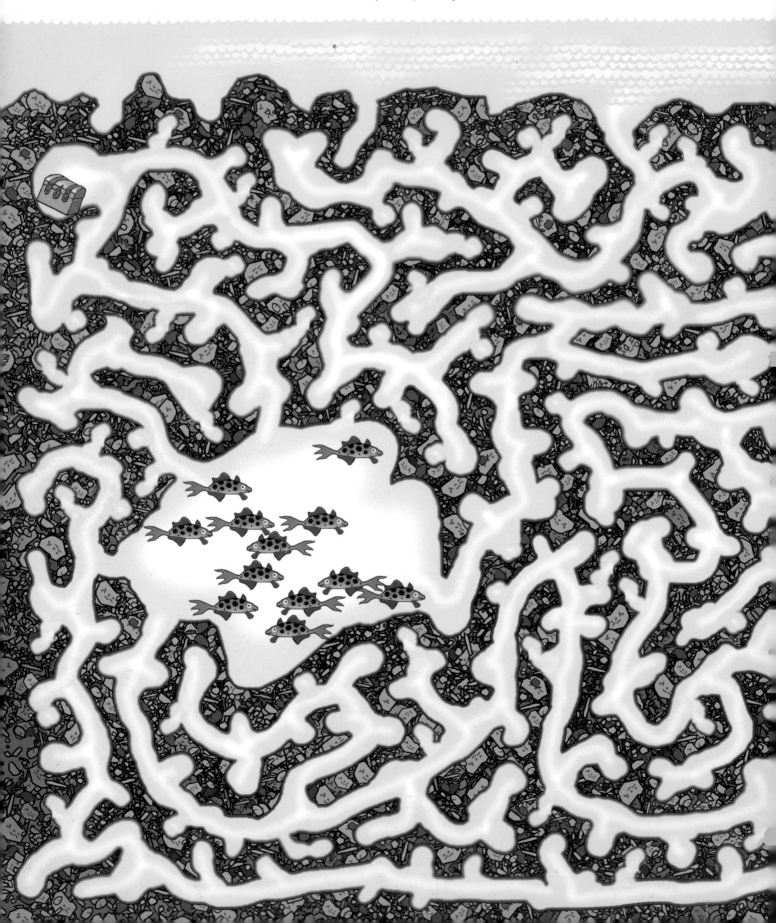

13. Cod You Find The Differences?

The males and females are similar, but there are some differences. Can you spot them?

Male Fish   Female Fish

14. Hermit Home

These five hermit crabs must each find a new home. And they are fussy about where they live! How many crabs will not find their perfect home?

c. This crab will only live in stripy shells, and they must have spikes.

b. This crab only goes into pointy shells, as long as they are pink!

d. This crab is looking for a spotty shell and she hates green!

a. This crab only goes into shells of the same colour, and they must have a pointy end.

e. This crab is not fussy. She just wants a light-coloured shell.

15. Sea Snails

These snails move slowly. How fast can you make it through the maze, from one side to the other?

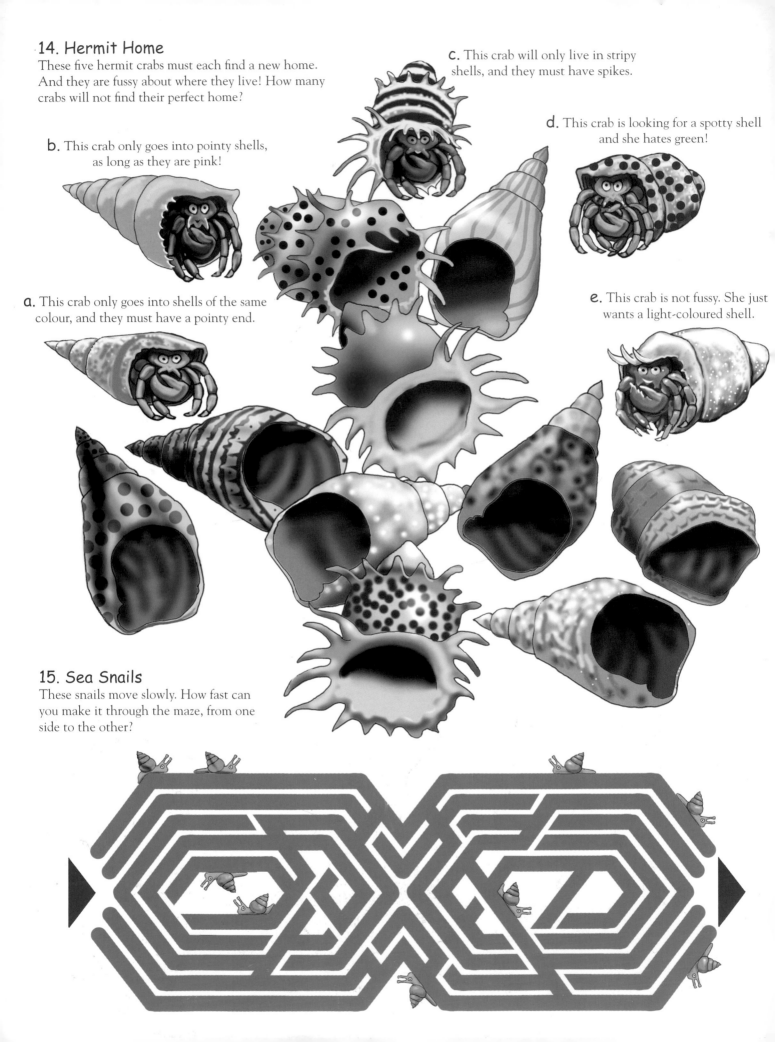

16. A Giant Starfish
Can you find your way through this starfish?
Don't let the bristles get in the way!

17. Eel Wiggle
These two eels are looking for each other.
Can you help find a path so one can wriggle through to the other?

18. Seahorse Parade

There is one seahorse in the box below that has the same features as the hidden seahorse. Can you guess which one it is?

19. Tight Squeeze

Can the eel squeeze through the blue channel to the opposite pond?

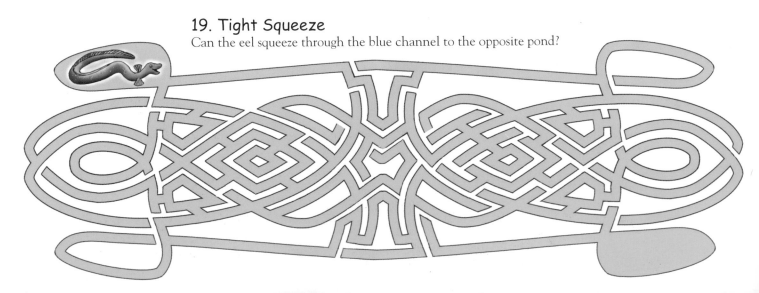

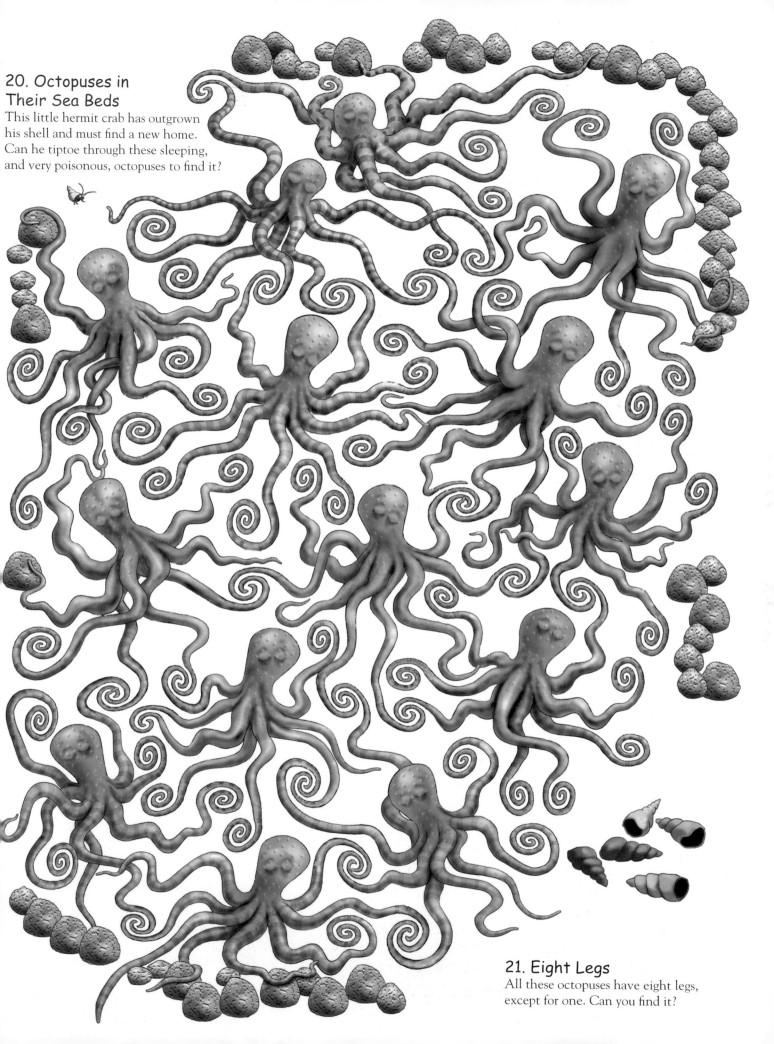

20. Octopuses in Their Sea Beds

This little hermit crab has outgrown his shell and must find a new home. Can he tiptoe through these sleeping, and very poisonous, octopuses to find it?

21. Eight Legs

All these octopuses have eight legs, except for one. Can you find it?

22. Clumsy Fishermen

Each of these fishermen has dropped
something into the water: a key, a pen, a hat
and a pair of glasses. Can you find each item?

23. Seabed Life

How many different types of sea creature can
you find in this picture? Some are very well
camouflaged, so look carefully.

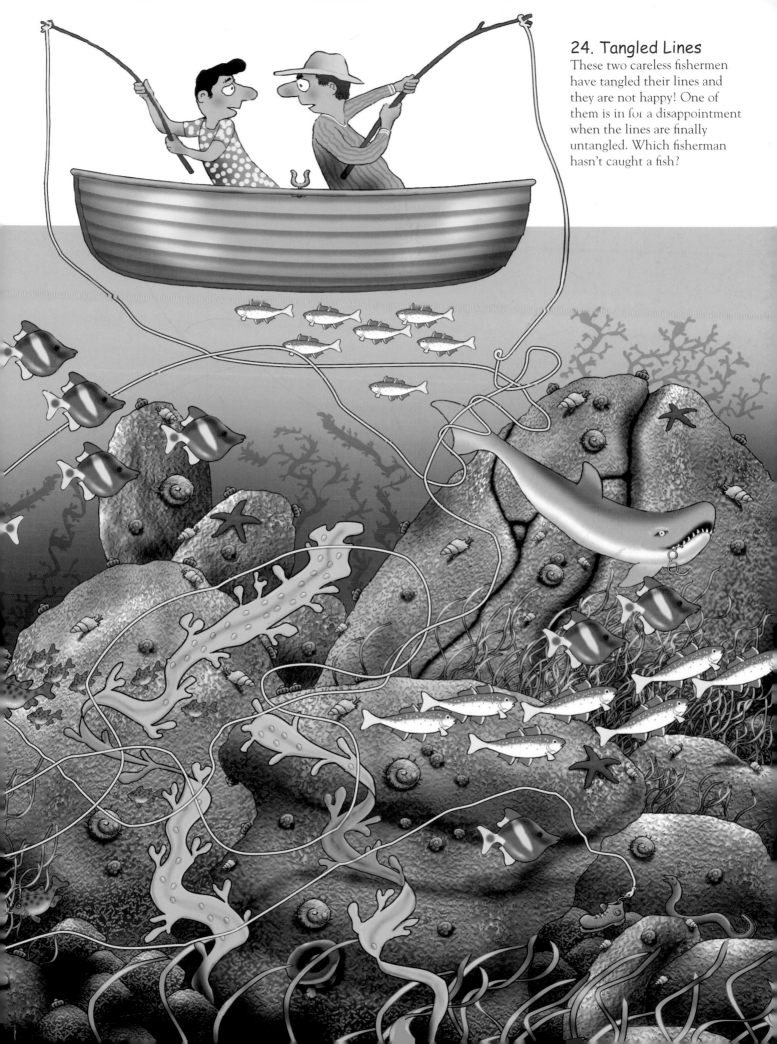

24. Tangled Lines

These two careless fishermen have tangled their lines and they are not happy! One of them is in for a disappointment when the lines are finally untangled. Which fisherman hasn't caught a fish?

25. The Giant Rainbow Cod

This rare Rainbow Cod also known as Labyrintus Fantasticus has the most unusual markings! So unusual in fact that they form a maze! Can you make your way from the lips to the tip of the tail?

26. Pee Wee Fish

After that big, difficult maze don't you just wish for a wincey one? Well, here it is! Help this little Pee Wee Fish find his way out of the maze.

27. Don't Eat Me!

One of these fish is poisonous! You can recognise it because it has a forked tail, a long snout, red eyes, yellow fins and a sharp spine. Which one is it?

28. Mirror Image

The two pictures of this underwater scene look roughly the same, but there are twelve differences! Can you find them?

29. Room to Move

Is it possible for the yellow octopus to squeeze through the maze to the purple octopus?

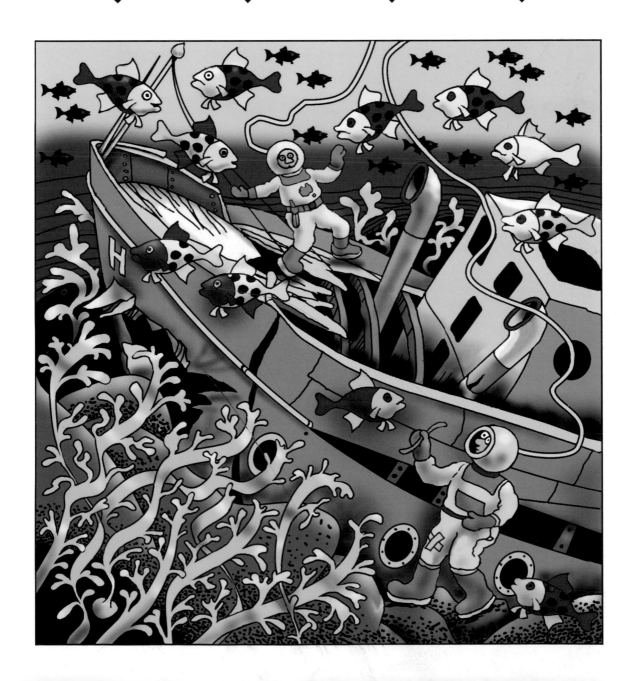

30. One Fish, Two Fish
These two fish prefer company to swimming alone in the big sea. Can you help one find the other?

31. Double Double Trouble

What a hard time this deep-sea diver is having. He is being attacked from every angle!
There are twelve differences between these two pictures. Can you spot them?

32. Ocean Litter

Shame on those who leave behind their rubbish in the sea! Worse still, some leave their old fishing hooks behind. Find all thirteen before they do any harm!

33. Floundering Flounder

This family of flounder is trying to get to the long, grassy patch of seaweed. There is a lot of rubbish in the way and they are having trouble getting there. Can you help them find a path over the sandy seabed?

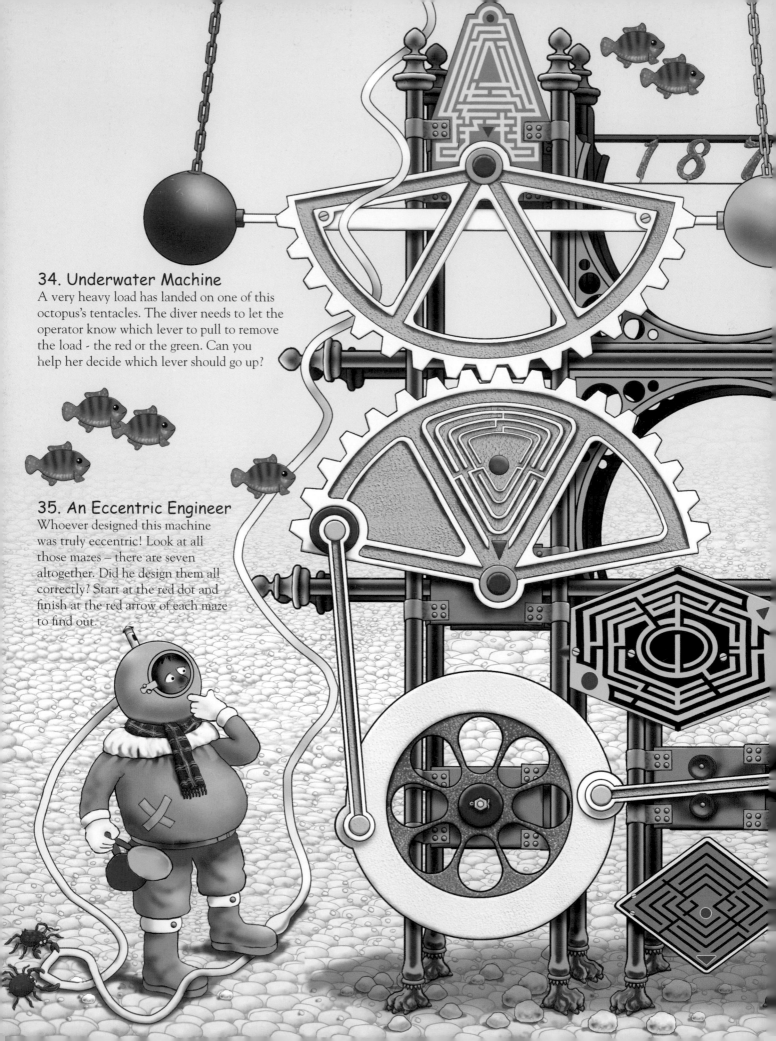

34. Underwater Machine

A very heavy load has landed on one of this octopus's tentacles. The diver needs to let the operator know which lever to pull to remove the load - the red or the green. Can you help her decide which lever should go up?

35. An Eccentric Engineer

Whoever designed this machine was truly eccentric! Look at all those mazes – there are seven altogether. Did he design them all correctly? Start at the red dot and finish at the red arrow of each maze to find out.

SOLUTIONS

1. Birds of the Sea
Follow the red line through the maze.

2. Shark Attack!
Follow the red line through the maze.

3. Endangered Starfish
The starfish with eight tentacles is circled in red.

4. Sea Life
There are more starfish than fish. There are 44 starfish and 29 fish. Did you remember to count the shark as a fish? The eel is circled.

5. Mind Your Step!
The thirteen differences have been circled.

6. Dinner Time!
Follow the red line through the maze.

7. The Lost World of Atlantis
Follow the red line through the maze.

8. Octopus Maze
Follow the red line through the maze.

9. The Right Suit
The grey suit cost $60.

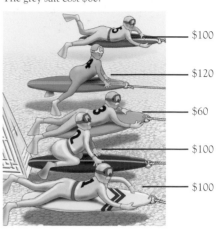

$100

$120

$60

$100

$100

10. Fish Racing
The fish marked '5' will finish the race in the middle.

11. Hidden Treasure
Follow the top red line through the maze.

12. Girl Meets Boy!
Follow the bottom red line through the maze.

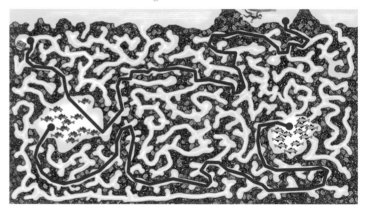

Male Fish   Female Fish

13. Cod You Find The Differences?
a. The males have red fins but the females have black fins.
b. The males and the females have different shaped tails.
c. The males have blue eyes but the females have red eyes.
d. The males have black spots but the females have blue spots.
e. There are fewer spots on the males than on the females, because there are no spots on the tails of the males.

14. Hermit Home
Only one crab will not find a new home. It is crab 'c'.

15. Sea Snails
Follow the red line through the maze.

16. A Giant Starfish
Follow the red line through the maze.

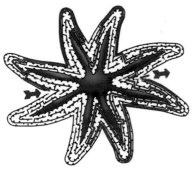

17. Eel Wiggle
Follow the red line through the maze.

18. Seahorse Parade
The seahorse that matches the hidden seahorse is circled.

19. Tight Squeeze
Follow the red line through the maze.

20. Octopuses in Their Sea Beds
Follow the red line through the maze.

21. Eight Legs
The octopus that doesn't have eight legs is circled. He has nine legs.

22. Clumsy Fishermen
The key, pen, hat and pair of glasses are all circled.

23. Seabed Life
There are 13 different varieties of sea creature.

24. Tangled Lines
The fisherman with the arrow pointing at him is the fisherman who has only caught a boot.

25. The Giant Rainbow Cod
Follow the black line through the maze.

26. Pee Wee Fish
Follow the red line through the maze.

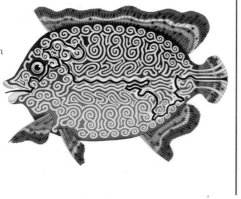

27. Don't Eat Me!
The poisonous fish is circled.

28. Mirror Image
The twelve differences are circled.

29. Room to Move
Follow the red line through the maze.

30. One Fish, Two Fish
Follow the red line through the maze.

31. Double Double Trouble
The twelve differences have been circled.

32. Ocean Litter
The thirteen hooks have been circled below.

33. Floundering Flounder
Follow the red line through the maze.

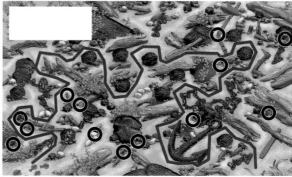

34. Underwater Machine
It works both ways! (See the diagram below for what happens when the red lever is pulled.)

35. An Eccentric Engineer
Follow the red line through each of the seven mazes.

Rolf Heimann was born in Dresden, Germany in 1940. In 1945, he witnessed the total destruction of his home city—which made him a lifelong opponent of war.

At age 18 he migrated to Australia. Over the next few years he worked his way around the country doing all kinds of jobs, including fruit-picking, labouring at railways and working in factories. Every spare hour was spent writing and sketching. Eventually, he settled in Melbourne, where he worked for printers and publishers before finally running his own art studio.

In 1974, Rolf sailed his own boat around the Pacific (and met his future wife, Lila, in Samoa), returning to Australia after two years to concentrate on painting, writing, cartooning and illustrating. He has now published over fifty books, including puzzle and maze books, junior novels and picture books. His books have travelled to dozens of countries and have sold millions of copies around the world.

Also by Rolf Heimann from Little Hare Books:

DRAGONMAZIA

DINOMAZIA

ROLF'S CORNY COPIA

PUZZLEMAZIA

CRAZY COSMOS

BRAIN BUSTING BONANZA

ASTROMAZE

ZOODIAC

ROLFS FLUMMOXING FLABBERGASTERS

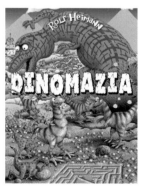
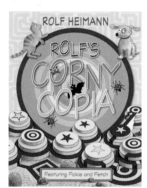

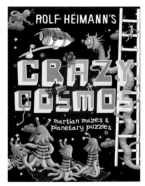

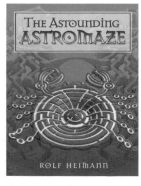
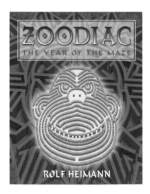